The Church Security Handbook

A Practical Guide to Protecting Your Congregation in Uncertain Times

VAUGHN BAKER

ISBN: 1979661774
ISBN-13: 978-1979661775

DEDICATION

This book is dedicated to the thousands of men and women who have committed themselves to protect the Body of Christ.

"Let us not become weary in doing good, for at the proper time we will reap a harvest if we do not give up."
– Galatians 6:9

CONTENTS

ABOUT THE AUTHOR

Vaughn Baker is the president of Strategos International, a Kansas City, Mo.-based firm that provides security training, consulting and executive protection services.

Vaughn has 20 years of experience in law enforcement including patrol, investigation, SWAT and special operations. He has trained thousands of school, health care, government, law enforcement and military personnel. Vaughn has also developed specialized intruder response curriculum for schools and churches. He has created some of the nation's leading training on behavior pattern recognition.

In addition, Vaughn serves as the director of security for a church of more than 6,000 in the Kansas City area, a position he has held for over a decade. This security team consists of two staff members and approximately 80 volunteers serving in armed and unarmed capacities.

ABOUT STRATEGOS INTERNATIONAL

Strategos has instructed more than 1,000 churches and ministries, including 25,000 staff and volunteers. In total, the firm has trained more than 125,000 people in the business, law enforcement and non-profit arenas. Strategos offers 10 different courses on church and ministry security for both staff and volunteers. The firm's philosophy is based on Matthew 10:16: "I am sending you out like sheep among wolves. Therefore be as shrewd as snakes and as innocent as doves." The company also offers numerous courses for schools, businesses and law enforcement.

Learn more at www.strategosintl.com.

INTRODUCTION

A Tale of two churches

Thank you for picking up "The Church Security Handbook." As a Christian, I am personally invested in the safety and security of the church.

My goal is to provide a realistic overview of the danger churches face and a solid outline of how to respond. This book provides the background you need to support and justify a trained, on-site response capability to board members, elders and your congregation.

There are some things this book cannot do. It can't replace the hands-on training that we and other organizations (including law enforcement) provide. Our hope is that you will take that next step so you can be confident and prepared.

If you get nothing else from "The Church Security Handbook," please understand this: Church security is not at odds with your ministry or biblical truth, but supports and complements both. A balanced, well-run security ministry helps your church *make an impact* instead of becoming a church *that is impacted.*

> There is no single right way to create a secure church environment. But however you do it, do something. Your congregation is depending on you.

Diverse approaches

As there are myriad denominations and expressions of faith, there are many approaches to church security. Some churches use unarmed volunteers whose focus is on awareness and dialing 911. Others use uniformed police officers. Some use teams that carry concealed weapons and are indistinguishable from any other member of the church (think undercover agents in the service of God).

Some churches have the benefit of including active or retired law enforcement and military personnel on their teams. Others are comprised 100 percent of lay volunteers.

Sometimes a church employee directs the ministry. Others are entirely operated by volunteers, but under the supervision of a pastor or staff member.

A tale of two churches

An Ohio newscast recently relayed the good news that multiple churches were receiving security training from law enforcement to help protect their congregations.

"In this day and age, who knows what could happen, who could walk through the front door?" said one pastor. "Bombings and violence in churches – it catches your attention."

We couldn't agree more. That's why we do what we do: Educate and equip churches, schools and businesses to be ready for the "What if?"

However, another pastor interviewed for the newscast said he was not worried and wouldn't be participating in the training. Why? He believes God will protect him and his flock. The pastor also believes violent acts haven't "happened in our churches and wouldn't for the most part." Finally, smaller churches are less likely to be targeted, he said.

I truly wish this pastor were correct and that we here at Strategos could close up shop. But we can't. And here's why.

It can happen here

There have been more than 1,000 violent incidents at churches since 1999 and a 600 percent increase in the last decade.[1] True, the statistical likelihood of it happening to your church is small. But the odds were equally small for the churches where people were killed. Statistics are cold comfort in those cases.

Does your church prepare for severe weather, fires or other natural crises? Do you prepare based on the small statistical probability that it could happen? If you did, no one would ever prepare for anything. Instead, we prepare for these events based on the impact they would have if they occurred. It's no different with preparation for violent intruders.

It can happen in rural areas

[2]Over half of active-shooter incidents at schools occur in rural areas (defined as communities of fewer than 10,000

---

[1] Source: Church Security Analyst Carl Chinn www.carlchinn.com/deadly-force-statistics.html; Also see Christianity Today: www.churchlawandtax.com/blog/2017/may/what-leaders-can-learn-from-violent-incidents-at-churches.html

[2] The Final Report and Findings of the Safe Schools Initiative, U.S. Department of Education and U.S. Secret Service, www2.ed.gov/admins/lead/safety/preventingattacksreport.pdf

people). These places can be as small as Nickel Mines, Pa. (population 43), where a gunman killed eight girls in a one-room Amish schoolhouse.

God can use our planning to protect us

I'm not a theologian, but the fact that 99% of us lock our doors indicates we believe God expects us to do something to protect ourselves. One of several verses that lends support to this is Proverbs 22:3:

"A prudent person foresees danger and takes precautions. The simpleton goes blindly on and suffers the consequences."

The newscast closed with a rebuttal from another pastor in the community. He spoke out against the idea that "it can't happen here."

"I think that it would be absolutely a travesty to take that position, because it can happen," he said.

Amen.

We'll pray that it won't, but will prepare in case it does.

CHAPTER 1
IT CAN HAPPEN HERE

Answering Objections to Church Security

When Strategos International began training churches in security, we expected most of the objections would come from people outside the church. We were wrong. The vast majority of negativity has come from people on the inside.

In the Western world, the words "church" and "security" don't seem to go together. After all, isn't the church by its very nature a sanctuary and refuge?

We have traditions of houses of worship being left unlocked 24/7 for people to pray and come and go as they please. Some still are.

In addition, we as Christians have a strong conviction that God is our protector and refuge. Does having a security presence somehow indicate a lack of faith? Many sincere pastors and church members believe this is the case.

Am I lacking faith?

Although I'm not a theologian or philosopher, I believe

some practical examples will dispel the idea that readiness and preparation represent a lack of faith in God's protection.

- Do you wear a seat belt?
- Do you lock your doors?
- Have you ever called the police? Or would you?

If you answer "yes" to any of these questions, do you lack faith in God? I certainly don't think so.

The Psalms are full of powerful promises about the protection of God. Yet the author of most of those Psalms, King David, was a renowned military leader. He still put on his armor and gathered his weapons while trusting in God for the outcome.

"A prudent person foresees danger and takes precautions. The simpleton goes blindly on and suffers the consequences." – Proverbs 27:12

We're called to faith and trust. But we're also called to action. We are not called to vigilantism or reaction, but to calm, reflective and sensible measures to safeguard our congregation.

Although no one can deny that violence is impacting churches, it's somehow tempting and comforting to think it could never happen to us.

We're too small. We're too rural. We're too inconsequential or uncontroversial. However, the data does not support these conclusions.

Yes, the odds of violence striking your church is small. The risk was minimal when a gunman murdered nine people at a Bible study in Charleston, S.C. The killer wasn't concerned about statistical probability – only taking lives.

What about rural areas? [3]More than half of violent incidents at schools occur in communities of less than 10,000 people.

We could ask, "What's the risk of an attack?"

[3] The Final Report and Findings of the Safe Schools Initiative, U.S. Department of Education and U.S. Secret Service, www2.ed.gov/admins/lead/safety/preventingattacksreport.pdf

But a better question is "What's the risk of doing nothing to prevent one?"

What happens when we fight back?

It's almost unthinkable that we would watch an attacker harm our spouse, children or grandchildren. We would do something, even if it was simply calling 911. Why should it be different with our congregation?

Surveys of people who fought an intruder found that their actions:

- Prevented injury or death
- Enabled the victim to escape
- Scared the intruder away

What happens if we don't fight back?

Pastors and church leaders want to see the good in everyone. I don't want to change this impulse. But we need look no further than the Bible to understand the depravity of human nature.

"The heart is deceitful above all things, and desperately wicked; Who can know it?" – Jeremiah 17:9

While we hope and pray for the best, we must prepare for the worst – especially if dozens, hundreds or thousands of people are counting on us to provide a safe environment.

Why would anyone want to attack your church? That's a good question. And it can't be answered with a good reason. Because there's nothing good or reasonable about someone killing innocent people.

Psychological profiles of active shooters reveal that:

• Many desire to set a new body count record.

• They understand they have 2-to-5 minutes to accomplish their goal.

• They plan to die or kill themselves in the course of the attack.

• They're motivated by hatred of Christians or someone inside the church.

• They suffer from severe psychological, social or emotional problems.

• They have planned the assault in detail.

• They're totally committed to the attack.

Given this level of opposition, failure to prepare can be devastating.

But we're peaceful people

I believe I've made a strong case, but a few people may not be convinced they're at risk. After all, you're a dues-paying member of the Chamber of Commerce. Everyone loves your church. Your food pantry has served thousands of meals in the community. Why would anyone take up arms against you?

Although you may not be aware of any physical enemies, the Bible is clear that we have a spiritual adversary who is hostile to our mission.

Second, given the profile of the assailant we just described, no rational motive for an attack is required. In fact, the motive is almost certainly irrational.

Third, innocent people are often caught in the crossfire when active shooters come on the scene. Domestic violence, for example, often spills over into the workplace or the church. An estranged spouse knows where his wife works or worships and shows up to cause devastation.

Are you convinced?

Church violence documented

The raw numbers don't tell the whole story, but they're an important place to start. From 1999-2017, there have been 1,150 deaths and injuries at churches due to attackers. The rate of violent incidents at churches has increased by nearly 2,400 percent since 1999. And it continues to rise.[4]

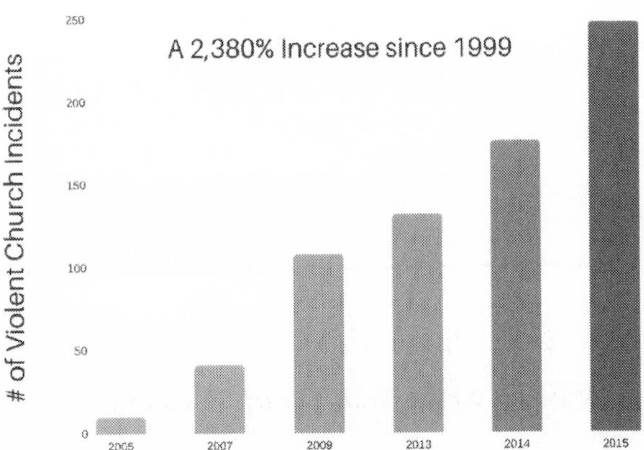

These incidents are not confined to a particular faith tradition. Certainly, more attacks happen in larger denominations, but they occur across the board.

[4] Source: Church Security Analyst Carl Chinn www.carlchinn.com/deadly-force-statistics.html; Also see Christianity Today: www.churchlawandtax.com/blog/2017/may/what-leaders-can-learn-from-violent-incidents-at-churches.html

What do those statistics look like in reality? Here are just a few examples.

Tennessee 2017

As church members left Burnette Chapel Church of Christ near Nashville, a gunman opened fire and killed Melanie Crow Smith in the parking lot. He then went inside and continued shooting, injuring seven people. A church member confronted the shooter, who accidentally shot himself in the leg during the struggle. That ended the assault.

Pennsylvania 2017

Mark Storms, a church member who was not part of the security team, intervened in a minor dispute that ushers were having with fellow church member Robert Braxton. Braxton became agitated when Storms approached him. Braxton threw a punch. Storms then fatally shot him in the chest in the middle of the worship service.

Idaho 2016

Tim Remington, pastor of Altar Church in Coeur d'Alene, was shot eight times in his church's parking lot by a psychologically disturbed man. Remington survived and has returned to the pulpit.

South Carolina 2015

Nine people were shot to death at a Bible study at Emanuel African Methodist Episcopal Church in Charleston by Dylann Roof, an avowed white supremacist.

Texas 2012

In Forest Hill, a convicted felon under the influence of narcotics drove his vehicle through a church entrance on a Sunday afternoon. He then beat the pastor to death with an electric guitar and severely injured a custodian.

Washington State 2010

In Federal Way, Charles and Carol Parsons attended a counseling session at Calvary Lutheran Church. When conflict arose, the husband pulled a pistol from his jacket and shot his wife dead.

Arkansas 2010

Lillian Watson, 80, was a volunteer at Central United Methodist Church in Wynne. She apparently interrupted a burglary when she went to the church for supplies. The burglar beat her to death with a cross from the altar.

North Carolina 2009

An estranged boyfriend shot and killed Jammie Shatel Street at St. August Missionary Baptist Church in Fuquay-Varina. She was dropping off her children at the church daycare.

We could fill books with details of these incidents. But it's not necessary to make the point: Bad things happen to good people in good places.

Churches: In the bull's eye

We've established that it's wishful thinking to believe it can't happen here. But there's more: Churches are in fact targets – and worse than that – soft targets.

Practical reasons for this truth:

• Churches contain lots of people, from a few dozen to a few thousand.

• The vast majority of people are facing away from the entrance where an attacker would enter. Often, no one's watching the back door.

• People are sitting close together with no quick means of escape.

Are you convinced?

The threat is real. Odds are that it won't happen to you. But no one gets to choose whether they'll become a statistic. What you can choose is whether or not to prepare in advance for the low-probability, high-impact event that will forever answer the question, "Is our church a safe place to worship?"

Personal Inventory

• What false beliefs have you, your church or your board harbored about the risk of church violence?

• Who in your church would benefit from the information in this chapter?

• What objections to church security do you need to overcome in your congregation?

CHAPTER 2
THE REAL PURPOSE OF TRAINING
Who Will Be the First to Respond to an Intruder?

When you're in trouble, what do you do? You call the police, right?

Good answer. Certainly, if there is an intruder at your church, home or business, you should call the police. However, dialing 911 is not magic. You'll talk to a dispatcher, provide information and then an officer will respond. But how far away are the officers? And how long will it take them to arrive?

And, more importantly, what kind of damage can be done in the 4-20 minutes it takes law enforcement to get there?

Like it or not, the people in the building during an intrusion are the first responders. What they do – or don't do – will make the difference in who lives or dies that day.

What are the benefits of preparation?

• It can prevent or stop violent and criminal activity, save lives and prevent injury.

• It can deter people bent on causing harm because they see that your church is prepared.

• It can prevent the long-term psychological and emotional damage that accompanies violence at church.

> Preparation cannot guarantee that nothing bad ever happens at your church. But it can certainly improve the odds.

Again, there is no guarantee that even the best-trained team will be able to stop all violence. But the odds go up when we're prepared.

We train for trouble with the goal of preventing it

Sorry to disappoint anyone, but our purpose is not to train your team to develop the skills of a law enforcement officer overnight. Our purpose, at least initially, is to learn how to understand human beings with the goal of de-escalating conflict.

In other words, you don't need to learn how to fight, but how to avoid getting into one. The vast majority of physical conflicts can be avoided by learning to de-escalate.

This concept can be difficult for some people to embrace. And these are exactly the people you do not want on your church security team.

This help is not wanted

• **Trigger-finger Tom** is excited about the Second Amendment, the NRA and shooting ranges. He can't wait for some "real life" experience with guns. Avoid Tom at all costs.

• **Macho Mike** joined the security team to boss people around and look cool wearing an earpiece like the Secret Service guys on TV. He's a fight waiting to happen. Thanks, but no thanks.

Pride is the default disqualifier from involvement in a church security team.

• **Insecure Ed** tries to hide his general lack of self-confidence through egotistically asserting himself over others. Ed needs counseling, not a license to carry or kill. I remember asking a security team applicant why he wanted to join. He said he was bullied in school and swore it would never happen again. This resolve, stemming from past insecurities, was certainly not the proper motivation to carry a firearm on our watch.

The ideal member is someone who has nothing to prove, cares about people and is most happy when she goes home without a confrontation that Sunday.

At Strategos, the theme that motivates our training is *Capability Breeds Humility*. This means competent, secure, individuals will be the best security team members. They're relaxed and confident because they've been trained and know what to do. They're comfortable in their own skin and don't need to prove anything. They're not excited about fighting, but will do it if necessary.

Now, back to why we train.

Normalcy bias

Our brain likes things to be routine, predictable and non-threatening. When disruptive events occur, we often fall prey to a psychological state known as normalcy bias.

Normalcy bias causes us to irrationally dismiss overt threats and real danger. We concoct bizarre interpretations of reality such as:

• Gunshots are cars backfiring or fireworks.

• A fistfight or man waving a weapon is part of a church drama.

• People running and shouting are part of a church drama.

Of course this sounds ridiculous when we're not under pressure. But in the heat of the moment, normalcy bias is often our default mode. It causes people to underestimate, minimize and rationalize a crisis. It's part of a subconscious belief that, since something has never happened to us, it cannot happen and is not happening.

Normalcy bias has led to deadly consequences. The good news: We can overcome it if we understand it and discipline our minds to perceive reality.

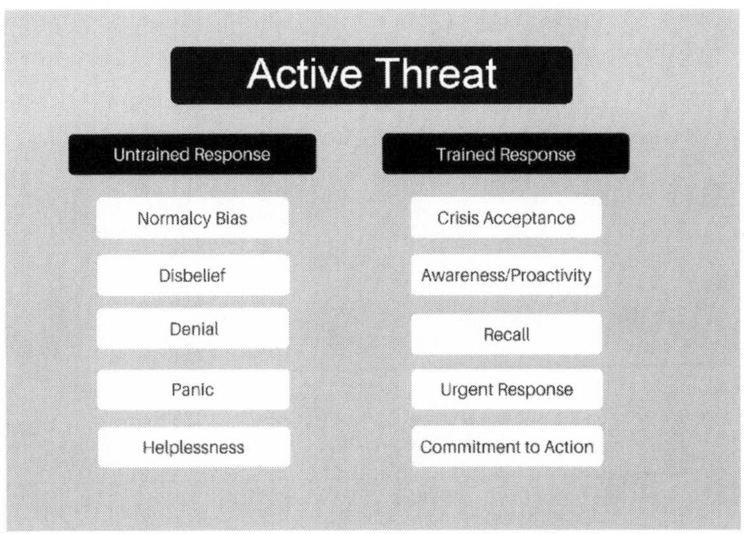

Active Threat matrix: Look at the difference training makes.

Personal Inventory

• How does understanding that your staff or members of your congregation will be the first responders to a crisis change the way you think about security?

• The goal of a security ministry is to defuse conflict before it begins. How should this affect the volunteers and/or staff members you invite to join your security team?

• Training is a critical component of a security ministry. Do you or your church have the resources to train staff and volunteers?

CHAPTER 3
SELECTING AND TRAINING YOUR TEAM

Capability Breeds Humility

When it comes to creating a security ministry, one size does not fit all.

While the mission of your church cannot be compromised, the style and type of your security ministry is highly flexible.

Here are just a few examples:

- An unarmed security team
- An armed, uniformed security team (such as off-duty officers)
- An armed, plain-clothes security team
- An all-volunteer security team
- A combination staff/volunteer security team
- A combination of any of the above

It's also critical to understand that a trained security team is only one part of an overall strategy. Training staff and volunteers (including parking teams, greeters, ushers, deacons and elders) to have a security mindset is the most important and first improvement you can make to increase safety and security.

> Every ministry needs a security mindset.

Security is not a task for someone else, but for everyone. Ushers and greeters – in particular – need to be alert for anyone or anything that seems out of the ordinary. When they see something, they need to say something – right then – not next week.

Children's ministry volunteers need to be trained to release children only to designated adults and not to anyone who claims to be Jacob's uncle.

Sometimes, even small changes can yield big dividends. Traditionally, ushers and greeters all sit down during the service with their back to the auditorium door. What if one or two stayed in the room, but took an alert posture?

It takes all team members, working together, to develop an effective security approach. You want layers of security, not a lone watchman.

In this diagram, each volunteer identified has a role in security.

Biblically speaking, we're talking about caring for the flock.

If the word "security" bothers you, then categorize this idea under the umbrella of pastoral care. Keeping people from being killed is definitely a caring gesture.

Friendly fire is never friendly.

Armed teams: Proceed with caution

If your team is going to be armed, its members must be trained. And this means more than having a concealed-carry permit. Concealed-carry training gives instruction in protecting yourself and your home. It is not oriented toward using a weapon in a public, high-traffic environment such as a church.

It's better not to have weapons than to put them in the hands of people who are unequipped to use them in a public setting. It will likely result in more deaths, not fewer, than if no weapons were present. The only way to create this kind of competency is through repeated professional training, and I'm not talking about merely spending time at the shooting range.

Beyond professional competency, what else do you look for in someone you are entrusting with a firearm?

- Do they love God?
- Do they love people?
- Do they pass the character test?
- Do you know them – really know them?
- How long have they been around?
- Can they pass a background check?

Those are a few places to start.

Training your team

Once you've selected a team of humble, reliable men and women, the next task is training (we mentioned background checks, right? You do that, right?). And please understand that training is not a one-and-done activity. It must be ongoing. When new team members join, they must be trained. Veterans need to be refreshed.

Capability Breeds Humility.

So what are the competencies you should train your team on? In a short book like this, we can't be comprehensive, but here are some key factors.

Body language: What does it indicate?

Team members need to be able to recognize body language that is out of the ordinary.

In interpersonal communication classes, it's often taught that 80 percent of communication is non-verbal. It's equally true when it comes to security.

We use an acronym JDLR to illustrate this point. JDLR stands for Just Doesn't Look Right. Please understand, this has absolutely nothing to do with age, ethnicity, religion or gender. It has everything to do with the person's general countenance, an awkward manner of dress (that might be concealing a weapon) and their level of social engagement.

All of us have a God-given "Spidey sense" about these things. The question is: Are we going to acknowledge it or rationalize and ignore it? We certainly do not want to judge a book by its cover, but we need to be aware of JDLR factors. We don't want to be paranoid *or* turn a blind eye to something that's concerning. Listen to your internal Spidey.

Engage everyone, but especially JDLR individuals

If an individual seems disoriented or anxious, give him a warm greeting. And not just one. The more people engaging with him, the better. This level of personal attention may deter someone who has come to cause harm. This is similar to deterring shoplifters: If they know people are watching, they leave.

It may also dissuade someone who is planning on self-harm. On the church security detail where I serve in the Kansas City area, our team noticed a JDLR individual. We talked with him, greeted him and observed him. We were convinced he meant no harm, but were still concerned about his condition. We asked one of the pastors to follow up before the person left the building.

The pastor met with the man, who confided he was planning to kill himself after the service. Instead, he put his faith in Jesus Christ. When you consider that real-life story, how important is awareness? We're not only talking about security, but ministry.

Reach out and touch someone

Although our natural tendency may be to steer clear of JDLR individuals, we need to engage them. This starts with a handshake and a pat on the back. Done correctly, this can determine if the individual is carrying a weapon (learn more from our online virtual training or live on-site training). We call this "aggressive friendliness."

Words matter

What's the best resolution to a conflict? Stopping it before it starts.

This can be summed up with a proverb:

> A gentle answer turns away wrath, but a harsh word stirs up anger.
>
> – Proverbs 15:1

The late Steven Covey popularized the phrase, "Seek first to understand, then to be understood." Have you ever felt that someone sincerely tried to understand your position? It's a rare but beautiful thing. Not only is it the right thing to do, it also defuses potential conflicts. Here's a summary of the approach we recommend:

- Listen
- Empathize
- Evaluate
- Request (or ask questions)
- Summarize

Listen

This means close your mouth and open your eyes. Make eye contact. The goal is not to wait until the other person finishes talking so you can blurt something out.

Empathize

The person, whether he is rational or not, is likely experiencing some sort of pain. Put yourself in his shoes.

Evaluate

Silently assess the situation.

Request

Find out what the person is seeking. Does she want prayer? A meeting with someone? Does he want to meet his estranged spouse, who filed a restraining order against him?

Summarize

Restate what you believe the person is feeling and wanting. "What I'm hearing you say is … ."

In many cases, this exercise alone can lower someone's anxiety level from 10 to 5 and defuse the conflict.

Phrases to avoid:

- "Hey you, come here!"
- "Calm down!"
- "I'm not going to tell you again!"
- "Because I said so!"

In general, avoid any phrase that ends with an exclamation point!

Instead, use genuine questions and engaging statements.

- "Hi. Is there anything I can help you with today?"
- "Let me see if I understand where you are coming from."
- "What could I do to help?"

Recognizing and responding to disruptive individuals

We've addressed the importance of gently yet proactively engaging someone who is either a JDLR or appears to be carrying a weapon. However, it's important to understand

It's better not to have weapons than to put them in the hands of people who are unequipped to use them in a public setting.

that all armed individuals are not equal. These range from people who are legally licensed to carry a concealed weapon to someone with criminal intent.

Who's carrying a concealed weapon? You can't always know, but some telltale signs are:

• Clothing that's inappropriate for the weather or occasion (an overcoat in July).

• A jacket that fits unevenly and swings like a pendulum with each step.

• Someone who repeatedly touches a likely location of a concealed weapon.

• Someone who tries to conceal adjusting a weapon when their body position changes (for example, moving from sitting to standing or vice versa).

• Someone walking with a gated stride or a slightly-clipped arm swing because the weapon hinders their normal movement.

Only a trained security team member should confront an armed individual. First of all, we can't make assumptions about why someone is armed. She may be an off-duty police officer. He may have a concealed carry license. Or he may be intent on killing someone.

If the person has a legitimate reason to carry a weapon, and you don't want weapons in the building, then they won't object to locking it up in their car. If the person in question is an off-duty or plain-clothes law enforcement officer, then their presence should be welcomed.

The goal is to avoid a confrontation and putting someone who is "packing heat" in a defensive position. You don't want that person to feel cornered and desperate.

What's the next step if an armed individual is a person of concern and appears ready to combust? A "how-to" for this scenario is beyond the scope of this book – or any book for that matter. The shortest answer is that professional training and practice is an absolute essential. Apart from that, chaos is likely to erupt if an untrained person approaches someone who is armed and JDLR.

Many protestors want attention and drama – the more the better.

Protestors

Although demonstrators are rarely hazardous to your health, they can be hazardous to your reputation if you respond improperly to their provocations.

A group based in the Midwest protests churches and even the funerals of soldiers. They're known for enticing counter-protestors to throw a punch – then suing them for everything they've got.

Even well-intentioned souls who bring coffee and donuts to protestors can end up embroiled in a confrontation with a toxic demonstrator. And that's what will make the news.

Inventory

• What are the advantages and disadvantages of armed security teams vs. unarmed security teams?

• What could you do this month to begin engaging your key volunteers – ushers, greeters, parking teams – to begin developing a mindset of awareness and security?

• Is there currently anyone in your congregation whose job is to be alert and aware on Sunday mornings or at other key times?

CHAPTER 4
LOCKDOWN

Better safe than sorry

When you listen to the news, there's a lockdown somewhere in the United States every week. A typical example is that gunshots are heard near a school. Just to be safe, they batten down the hatches.

When it comes to instituting a lockdown, things have gotten serious. We know, or think, there is an intruder nearby or in the building wishing to disrupt or do harm.

Undoubtedly, some may object to a lockdown. Why make a fuss? What if word gets out that you had a lockdown?

First of all, doing the right thing is often unpopular. But conversely, what if word got out that you had a chance to protect your children and did nothing? What impact would this have on:

- The lives of those affected?
- Their relationship with the church?
- Your church's relationship with the community?

> My advice: Get trained. Get informed. Do the right thing and let God handle the complaints.

The goal of lockdown is:

• Prevent the intruder from getting access.

• Secure the building or rooms within it.

• Remove vulnerable people from a threat.

• Isolate the threat.

• Allow for an accurate accounting of the people in each room.

• Depending on the situation, evacuate people from the threat in an organized manner.

There are two types of lockdowns:

1. Locking the outside doors to keep an intruder out.

2. Locking inside doors (classrooms, meeting rooms, hallway access doors) to protect people from an intruder already inside.

Getting from normal mode to lockdown mode doesn't happen by accident and will not happen effectively without training.

Decisions that must be made ahead of time include:

• Who determines when to institute a lockdown and how it will be communicated?

• What should you do once the doors are locked?

• Who determines and announces when the lockdown is over?

When lockdown fails

In a worst-case scenario, an intruder may enter a building before a lockdown can be fully implemented.

A common method of instruction, often advocated by the federal government, is called Run, Hide, Fight. Something is better than nothing. But at Strategos, we have devised what we call the *3 Out Response Model.* It's different from Run,

Hide, Fight in several respects. The three components of it are:

- *Lock Out*
- *Get Out*
- *Take Out*

One of the most important differences is that *the 3 Out Response Model* is non-linear. That means there is no particular order of which "out" should be taken first. You choose the best response based on your location and the nature of the threat.

Lock Out

This means what is says. Lock the door. Keep the intruder from getting access. Advanced (and simple) locking mechanisms, such as the Barracuda, can make it nearly impossible for an intruder to enter a room. Don't be satisfied with a locked door alone. Create redundancy by locking, layering and reinforcing entrances.

Get Out

This means, when it's prudent, leaving the building and the source of the threat. Fleeing the building may not always be the best option, however, if there's the possibility of a shooter outside. This can also mean evacuating an open area to get to a lockable room. In that instance, you're both *getting out* and *locking out.*

Take Out

This means fighting the intruder by using whatever means are at your disposal. It could be classroom scissors, a fire extinguisher, a music stand, wooden blocks, chairs – anything that can stop the attacker.

Of the three responses, *Take Out* is the most controversial. We oppose vigilantism and unnecessary violence. But when confronted by a hostile intruder committed to your death, what are your options? You can accept your imminent demise and the murder of all those around you, or you can do something. Are there people in your life worth living for? If so, you owe it to them to fight.

The key to the *3 Out Response Model* is that it is not sequential. In other words, you do not first attempt to *Lock*

Out, then attempt to *Get Out* and finally fight (*Take Out*). You use any and all of these tactics when necessary.

The 3 Outs in action

It's not the Sunday morning you hoped for. A member of your parking team radios that a husband with a restraining order just pulled into the parking lot at your church, where his wife worships. Their three children are in class in the nursery.

Mr. Smith knows he's not supposed to be on the property and he's been warned. He's had a few run-ins with the police, including arrests for domestic violence.

A staff member dials 911.

Smith makes a bee-line for the nursery and walks briskly past the check-in station, ignoring the protests of volunteers who ask him to stop.

It's too late to *Lock Out* the entire building. But with quick action, the classroom teacher locks the door and moves the children outside the view of the window, then turns off the lights.

Smith screams and pounds on the door, but it's not going to budge. Frustrated, he tries to find his wife. Warned that

Mr. Smith was in the building, Mrs. Smith sought refuge behind a locked door in the church office. She decided to *Get Out* of the open auditorium.

This leaves Smith wandering the hallways looking for his estranged spouse. Security team members calmly approach him, "Hey, can I help you with anything Mr. Smith?"

He knows his cause is hopeless. But what will he do? Fight or flee? And if he fights, is he armed? The police are responding, but they've not arrived.

The security team speaks to him in a calm, reassuring tone.

"Mr. Smith, how can we help you?"

"I just want to see my kids!"

"I'm so sorry. You know there are legal issues involved here and it's out of our hands. I can't imagine how hard this is for you."

Smith begins to weep. And moments later, the police arrive. They take care of the *Take Out*, but there's no struggle. Smith cooperates.

Do you get it? You could rewrite this story in many different ways and still employ *The 3 Out Response Model* to deal with the threat.

The model supplies three simple, memorable options. In a crisis, you choose the option(s) that make the most sense in your circumstance.

The importance of education and training

All of this starts with getting a plan on paper. But it cannot stop there.

> The best plan is worthless unless it's put into practice.

That means your team must:

- Know of the plan
- Understand the plan
- Be able be to implement the plan.

This can only happen through training. And lots of it.

This is true whether we're speaking of severe weather, a power outage, a fire or an active shooter. Planning, education and practice prevent chaos.

Inventory

- Do you currently have a lockdown plan?
- Do you have a crisis response plan for a fire or severe weather?
- If you have these plans, could your staff and volunteers implement them if a crisis happened this week?

CHAPTER 5
WHAT NOW?

Every Step Is Important. Take One Today.

If you've made it this far in this book, then you truly care about your congregation. I commend you.

But don't think you're finished. In fact, you've only just begun.

If possible, join us at one of our live trainings. We spend two days helping you understand all aspects of church security in our basic course. Further training is available, including 10 different courses for leadership, staff, volunteers and security teams. View all of our training dates at www.strategosintl.com/schedule.

If we're not already coming to a community near you soon, your church could host a training. That way, you not only benefit, but help other churches in your city. If neither of those options works, we have digital training available in online, USB or DVD formats for large and small groups.

Make the most of the resources you have. Something is better than nothing.

If none of this is possible, you can still do something.

Here are a few ideas to get started:

• Involve staff, ushers, greeters and parking lot teams in the ministry of awareness. The more people looking out for the common good, the better.

• Establish a security point person, whether staff or volunteer, who is available and engaged.

• Evaluate which doors are unlocked. Can any be secured to control access?

• Make sure you have fire and severe weather evacuation plans and a secure children's area.

• Church parking lots are the location of numerous crimes ranging from theft to murder. Make sure your parking area is well patrolled and brightly lit.

• Consider adding security cameras as a deterrent – and make sure they're working.

• Does your building have a basic alarm system? It should.

• Take an inventory of who has keys to your building. This is often a practice that is abused, with a dozen lay people having keys that they often copy and loan to others. Minimize the distribution of keys. If necessary, change the locks and start over.

• Finally, make sure all of your volunteers – regardless of the ministry they serve – pass a background check. Better safe than sorry.

Don't give up

When it comes to church security, it's easy to get a running start and then slow to a crawl. Each change and improvement requires perseverance, may need a budget and could face opposition.

Consider church security to be a marathon, not a sprint. Despite the effort, it's a race worth running. Security training is not "one and done." It's like everything else in ministry: ongoing.

If you ever find yourself thinking "we have arrived," then you're in jeopardy of a security failure. Pride comes before the fall. Preparedness is a journey, not a destination. Trends, threats, people and environments are always changing. Persevere on the journey of continuous improvement.

What is the alternative? What is the risk? What does it take to protect the flock in today's ultra-violent, dysfunctional and broken world?

Whatever it takes is what we must do.

Vaughn Baker

Strategos International

vaughn@strategosintl.com

888.569.5444

www.strategosintl.com

Made in the USA
Columbia, SC
16 March 2018